O BY BOBBY FLAY

y Flay's Boy Gets Grill: 125 Reasons to Light Your Fire!
Julia Moskin)

y Flay Cooks American: Great Regional Recipes with Sizzling New Flavors
Julia Moskin)

y Flay's Boy Meets Grill: With More Than 125 Bold New Recipes
Joan Schwartz)

Flay's From My Kitchen to Your Table
Joan Schwartz)

Flay's Bold American Food
Joan Schwartz)